YOU

by Mark Wilson

SAMUEL FRENCH

samuelfrench.co.uk

FOR AMATEUR PRODUCTION ENQUIRIES

UNITED KINGDOM AND WORLD
EXCLUDING NORTH AMERICA
plays@samuelfrench.co.uk
020 7255 4302/01

Each title is subject to availability from Samuel French,
depending upon country of performance.

Acting Editions

BORN TO PERFORM

Playscripts designed from the ground up to work the way you do in rehearsal, performance and study

---

Larger, clearer text for easier reading

Wider margins for notes

Performance features such as character and props lists, sound and lighting cues, and more

---

+ CHOOSE A SIZE AND STYLE TO SUIT YOU

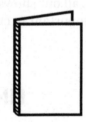

STANDARD EDITION

Our regular paperback book at our regular size

SPIRAL-BOUND EDITION

The same size as the Standard Edition, but with a sturdy, easy-to-fold, easy-to-hold spiral-bound spine

LARGE EDITION

A4 size and spiral bound, with larger text and a blank page for notes opposite every page of text. Perfect for technical and directing use

---

ABOUT THE AUTHOR

Mark Wilson is a writer and visual artist. His radio credits include *Talk* and the monologue version of *You* for BBC Radio 4. His most recent theatre credits include *Brief Encounter*, winner of the "Diez Minutos" Theatre Festival in San Miguel Di Allende, Mexico, and the stage version of *You*, winner of the 2015 Brighton Festival Award for Theatre, the Fringe Review Outstanding Theatre Award and the Argus Angel Five-Star Award. Mark is a writer for Longsight Theatre.

AUTHOR'S NOTE

This is Kathleen's story. The characters within it emerge from her imagination and her memory.

The play is written to be performed by two actors who remain on stage throughout the action. This facilitates the seamless changes of character and setting that are typical when that tumbled fusion of memory and imagination occur. The effect should be one of unbroken flow; a stream of consciousness.

Rather than provide detailed stage directions as to how these moments might be communicated to an audience, they are signposted in the text solely as changes of character name. It is my hope that directors and actors will engage their audience's imaginations in the story-telling process by developing their own means of indicating these "shifts".

Design:
The original Longsight Theatre production for the Brighton Festival involved the use of just two chairs and no props. Lighting changes from a basic state were minimal in order to enhance the sense of "unbroken flow" mentioned above. The only sounds were the commissioned pieces composed and performed by Benedict Taylor.

Mark Wilson

You was first performed by Longsight Theatre at the Brighton Festival in May, 2015, where it won the *Brighton Festival Award for Theatre, The Fringe Review Outstanding Theatre Award* and the *Argus Angel Five-Star Award.*

Cast:
Stephen Myott-Meadows
Kathryn O'Reilly

Directed by:
Sarah Meadows

Music composed and performed by:
Benedict Taylor

Adoption advisor:
Sue Bineham

The one-woman monologue version of *You,* first performed on BBC Radio 4 by Victoria Gould and from which the main text was developed, appears on page thirty-seven.

I am indebted to everyone at Longsight Theatre for the creativity, tirelessness and belief that they have brought to making this show happen. www.longsighttheatre.com

Mark Wilson

For Jill

And to Sarah, Rossie and Ste at Longsight Theatre – the
people who make things happen.

CHARACTERS

Two actors playing:

KATHLEEN – Forties.
JUNE – Kathleen's mother. Forties in Kathleen's recollections of her.
MARGIE – Frank's mother. Thirties.
VANESSA – Charlie's adoptive mother. Early thirties.

BILL – Kathleen's father. Forties in Kathleen's recollections of him.
CHARLIE – Kathleen's son. Thirties.
FRANK – The boy. Nineteen.
TOM – Charlie's adoptive father. Early thirties.

Scene One

KATHLEEN So today: Friday. Imagine. Him, coming here.

You still have the clothes, don't you; the ones they let you keep? Still in that drawer in the upstairs room, and the piece of faded blue card with his birth-weight and the time – blue for a boy.

The letters are in there too.

You. You broke your mother's heart, you did, Kathleen. Fifteen years old.

JUNE The shame.

KATHLEEN The way she said it it sounded like the plague.

You. You were an angel fallen from grace, clattering to the ground with just the same sound as all those grinny-toothed, school-uniform photos she'd gone round the house turning over, slamming down – broken glass across your face.

The shame.

That was the morning she found out, remember? She didn't guess; she knew. Making you tell her.

JUNE How many weeks late? Look at me. How many?

KATHLEEN Dragging at your arm to turn you round, hurting. You were never easy.

JUNE And now this. This. Fifteen years old. Well you're going to get rid of it, hear me, Kathleen?

KATHLEEN And there were your father's sad eyes, slowly pulled away when you met by awkward chance upon the stairs, or if he came suddenly into a room he'd thought was empty.

The way the opening door would shock you back from your dreaming down amongst the gas-fire colours, your shoulders hunching forward, hands fumbling in your lap to hide the slowly-swelling shape of you.

See him stand there for a moment, hesitant, as though wanting to speak, as though wanting for you both to speak as you had always done, but now neither of you able to find the words.

He'd sigh then, wouldn't he – turn back out the room more slowly than he had entered it. Your dad. That's all the memory you have of him now, that sad slow turning away.

Scene Two

BILL The worst part? It wasn't what you'd done: the falling pregnant. It's this new quiet between us, Kathleen. That's the worst part.

KATHLEEN My dad.

BILL There was the day I found out, coming home, the kitchen. You might have thought that that would have been it: the finding out. Your mother pushing at you, telling me:

JUNE We've got something to say, haven't we? Something to explain. Well go on, Kathleen.

BILL The way she wanted you to say it yourself.

JUNE Tell him what you've done.

BILL And when you couldn't, when you were crying so much and telling me you were "so sorry, Dad", her saying it for you.

JUNE I'm pregnant – go on. I've behaved disgustingly with some lad I hardly knew – some army lad.

BILL You might have thought that that was it, Kathy, but no. Being told wasn't the worst part. It's this quiet that's slid between us now like glass – thick. It wasn't silence. There was no anger in it for silence. Just quiet.

KATHLEEN The silence was between Mum and me. Remember?

BILL You two? Talk of being able to cut the air with a knife. You couldn't have dented it with a bloody shovel. Felt like trying sometimes, mind you. Silence? Loudest bloody silence I've ever heard.

Week after week of it till finally:

I can't bloody stand this.

JUNE And you think I can, do you? You think I can, her own mother? And you. You won't even–

BILL Won't what?

JUNE Tell her off. Get angry. Anything. Always left to me. Why's it always left to me?

BILL And say what, June?

What's left to say?

What's left?

KATHLEEN Shame – and sadness.

Shame and sadness became the places they retreated to then; separate, silent places. There was no rage. No bitter kitchen-table nights. Rage would have made it easier. Too easy. Rage would have given you something to rage against. But instead, her unforgiving, hall-clock silence pointing at you as you moved from room to room, its cold finger pushed back tight across your lips.

JUNE Quiet now; we'll say no more about it. It's all forgotten.

KATHLEEN So it was agreed, arranged. Remember? A place where they'd deal with everything: have the baby; come home. You would only be gone for a short while.

JUNE A holiday, that's what we'll say. She's gone to her aunt's for a holiday.

BILL There'd be no money

JUNE Wasted on taxis?

BILL But all that way, June love.

JUNE Well you'd better start early then, the pair of you.

BILL That morning. The three of us standing there in the narrow hallway at the foot of the stairs. She wasn't coming with us. She never said but I knew.

JUNE We'll see you in a bit, I suppose, your dad and me.

There then.

BILL Her, tying the knot of your headscarf. Her fingers difficult. The way she had to leave the knot half done, patting at it as though hoping it might somehow tie itself. Her lips tight.

JUNE There then.

BILL And when I looked back from the front gate–

KATHLEEN You must have thought she'd be standing at the window, see us go. No. But I remember you looking back.

BILL Sitting together there on the bus, your case on the seat between us – your things. Your things for going away. You know – never told you – but I started thinking back then at all those other bus rides.

KATHLEEN The time we went to Beadle Sands and I cut my foot on some glass.

BILL You didn't cry. The St John's man said you deserved an ice-cream.

KATHLEEN For being brave.

BILL And after, on the bus home, you said we should both have an ice-cream because I'd been brave too, you said. Four years old.

KATHLEEN And that Christmas, I was seven or eight, getting the bus into the town–

BILL –to buy a present for your mother.

KATHLEEN I chose a scarf. Blue with white dots.

BILL You'd saved up and you chose her a scarf.

And when I took you to Dale Park Farm–

KATHLEEN –lifting me up to pat the horse.

BILL And the evening we went to the King's Theatre. The Hopwood Light Opera Society: "Extracts from the Classics".

JUNE We can't afford it, Bill.

BILL But I wanted you to hear the tunes, Kathleen.

JUNE Bill, we can't afford it.

BILL You'd been unwell and we had to change buses twice, but I wanted you to hear the tunes.

You, asking to know why your mother wasn't coming with us and then not wanting to go if we weren't all going together. You, crying, telling me you wanted to be a family. Then missing the second bus and almost being late and you saying we shouldn't have come at all and me beginning to wish we hadn't.

People having to stand to let us into our seats and you coughing and people turning round and the lights going down and it starting.

And your face. Your face, Kathy.

KATHLEEN My dad.

That's all the memory you have of him now, that sad slow turning away.

And later, years later, when you had moved away and come back alone to pack her things – after the funeral. It was all still there, that same tight-lipped struggle for a self-acceptance she called respectability. There in the anxious precision of the dried-flower arrangement, in the order of the animals made of glass. It was there, in the correctness of things.

Well that was why it had happened, wasn't it: the thought of being incorrect; the excitement, the reckless anger of it? But it was so awful. That boy.

Some lad I hardly knew – some army lad.

Scene Three

FRANK And didn't I look the part? Didn't I just look the dog's bollocks? Forty-eight-hour pass, marching down Heath Street in my uniform, kit bag over my shoulder. Nineteen. Home. Didn't tell her I was coming, my mum. A surprise. Not as big as the one she had for me though.

MARGIE You'll have to sleep downstairs, Frank.

FRANK Just like that: slam. First thing she said to me. Not:

MARGIE Hello, Frankie.

FRANK Or:

MARGIE Everyone, it's Frank. Frankie's home.

FRANK Just:

MARGIE You'll 'ave to sleep downstairs.

FRANK The baby had my room.

All that bloody way home, a forty-eight hour pass and that's the welcome I get?

Later she said how they were sorry but that I had to understand.

MARGIE Should have told us you were coming.

FRANK It'd been a shock–

MARGIE –opening the door and finding you there.

FRANK They were a family now: her new man and the baby.

MARGIE You have to see that, Frank.

FRANK See it? 'Course I could bloody see it. And I could feel it. By the evening I just couldn't wait to get out.

MARGIE But where?

FRANK I don't know where. Just out, anywhere. I'll let myself in. Slamming the door.

MARGIE Frank?

FRANK Hearing her–

MARGIE Frankie?

FRANK –and wanting so badly to turn round and go back – so badly, but not half as bad as wanting to punish her by walking away.

I walked. Just kept walking, wanting to get away from them. Wanting to get away from where there was nowhere to be. I told her that. Wanting to get away from where I wasn't wanted, and I wasn't. I told her that too.

And somehow then, there I was, standing in Castle Street, half-way down:

The Regal. Dance night at The Regal. A fiver in my pocket and a packet of Woodbines.

I'd walked away from where I wasn't wanted and walked straight into her: the girl at the dance. And like no other time since I was a kid – or perhaps even never before – I felt myself belong. And feeling it so strongly I began to feel just how much I didn't really belong anywhere at all.

That's what made it so important, what made her so important – the girl at the dance.

And it was all like a film, wasn't it: me one side of the dance hall, you on the other, looking across? You smiling at me. Me looking round pretending I'd thought that you was smiling at someone behind me then turning back and pointing at myself.

KATHLEEN Made me laugh.

FRANK Just like a film. Remember, they had one of those sparkly ball things turning on the ceiling? Spots of light spinning all over everything.

KATHLEEN It's snowing.

FRANK That's what you said – the first thing you ever said to me:

KATHLEEN It's snowing.

FRANK And I watched as you held out your hands either side to catch the flakes, eyes tight shut, head slightly back like you could feel it on your face, and I couldn't speak.

And the way you laughed then, your fingers playing in the light, catching, catching it. The way you laughed.

And your arms tight round me holding on and me holding on. And that feeling of us filling up the room so that it became our room and everybody there had only space enough to stand round its edge. Our room. And – daft this – but it all felt so much like something I could keep, something I could hold on to and keep so that it would never be lost.

Then walking you home, hugging you in tight against the rain, telling me your name:

KATHLEEN Kathleen.

FRANK –that you were eighteen and worked in a chemist's, got a half-day on Thursdays. And your road sparkling the way the dance floor had sparkled. You were quieter, remember? Leaning into me. And I was quiet too and we stopped before we got to your house.

KATHLEEN Quickly then, before I go in.

FRANK Tomorrow, yes? Ten-thirty. My train leaves at two.

KATHLEEN If I can.

FRANK Ten-thirty.

KATHLEEN If I can, Frankie. Yes. Yes, I'll be there.

FRANK Heard your gate, your front door. Like a film. And me, I'd never been happier, not ever in my life. That's what you made me: happier than I'd ever been. Walked back through the sparkling road, all the long way home.

Kathleen.

Ten-thirty.

Raining. Soon as I saw you, I knew you weren't eighteen, sixteen more like – fifteen even.

And even before you reached me, I could see that something had gone from last night, something about that easy laughter as you'd stood there with your hands outstretched, catching snow. It was like the tide had gone out and there was only this shyness left behind. Snow? Don't make me laugh.

The rain had flattened your hair and your feet were wet in your wet shoes. Your thin legs. You looked smaller and I felt as though I'd been caught lying to myself. There's nothing you can keep, not for ever there isn't.

Didn't say anything, couldn't. Just that wanting to hold on to you, but not because it was you I wanted to hold but because by holding you I thought I might get back that thing that wasn't there anymore: us confident; us laughing, and you with your hands outstretched – get it all back.

And that's how the talk began: going somewhere quiet, away; that place near Dale Park or somewhere, anywhere. And you asking me why and I didn't know why but that I knew I wanted to be with you somewhere where we could just – I don't know.

Felt you leaning into me again like the night before. Started walking more quickly and my face was hot and a feeling in me of things rushing.

KATHLEEN Just holding,

FRANK Yes, just holding.

The wet grass.

KATHLEEN There was something hurried about him that surprised me. I remember that.

It was as though by having said, "yes", I'd reduced to nothing the very thing he'd seemed to have spent so long wanting for: a feeling of belonging. By saying "yes" I'd turned it into something spoilt and best done with quickly.

And in that moment where I thought I'd find a sense of being wanted, there was only the wanting for him to finish.

I'd spoilt it. He didn't say, but that's what I'd done. You were never easy, and now this. This.

And after, everything crushed – the grass, my clothes. "The dress is new," I told him. He told me he was in love.

Some lad I hardly knew – some army lad.

There are houses built there now.

Scene Four

KATHLEEN So, today. Two hours. Imagine.

The little clothes. Sometimes I go into the upstairs room, just to look, to touch. It's where I've put the letters, next to the piece of faded blue card with his birth-weight and the time – blue for a boy.

The letters.

The first one. Six weeks ago.

I thought it was one of those lost-children charity appeals – I knew the language well enough: *I am writing on behalf of a young friend who is trying to trace a relative with whom he has lost touch.*

I was all set to throw the silly thing away, remember, my mind already gone on to other things? Then I saw a date, the name of a town. This town.

My hand pushed, sudden, tight across my mouth as though about to be sick, shaking.

Not me.

Trying to breathe.

No. They don't mean me. Just a coincidence, that's all. Just a stupid –

Sending out stuff like this. Not a thought to the damage it –

And the page fluttering in my fingers like something caught.

Can't be. Mustn't.

And then angry with myself. Ashamed. As though by wondering about him all those years, I'd somehow brought this about, this disruption, this interference. Well you shouldn't have. Hear me? Shouldn't have. All that thinking. All that telling yourself: *Today he's one year old.* And, *September: he'll be starting school this week. Today he's twenty-one, imagine.* And – and the hardest one: *Does he ever think of me?* Stupid. Stupid.

CHARLIE But I did.

KATHLEEN He does.

Thirty years.

You.

I replied, terrified, curious. Yes. Yes, I told the social worker, the young friend could write if he wanted to. No, I didn't know how I'd respond.

And the awful waiting.

His first letter. Three weeks, last Wednesday.

I'd somehow expected the writing to be like a child's – big felt-tipped letters sprawling my address. Not this, this man's writing.

Didn't open it at first, couldn't; just smoothed at the envelope as though the letters were in braille, the way I'd smoothed his hair, his cheeks. The feel of it. Can't be.

And:

CHARLIE How odd, writing to you.

KATHLEEN And I wrote back: "Odd, yes."

My dry tongue as I tried to lick the stamp. The catching in my stomach as I let the envelope fall away down into the letterbox. Wanting to get home. Feeling the years fall back, fall away. Feeling the years fall in on me. Wanting to cry.

It seemed the only thing to do then, didn't it, as soon as I got in; the only place to go? I sat on the floor of the upstairs room by the open drawer and for the first time I let it come back to me. Staring out across those years, I dared let it all come back to me again: the milky warmth; the tiny sleepy softness of him; those wide deep eyes holding me. Mine. The only time I'd ever really been in love, I told myself. All mine.

And after the birth, six short weeks of them bringing him in to be fed. Six weeks of them coming to take him away again afterwards, and my heart with him.

And then that day they didn't come for him – not straight away. That's how I knew: it will be today. Now. Giving me time; they were telling me by giving me time – warning me. And suddenly, suddenly so much to say to you; a lifetime of telling, of asking and listening. But still I never finished – oh, as if I ever could have finished.

There was no struggle. "We don't want him woken now, Kathleen," they told me. "That's it. Just need to show him to the couple who'll be taking him; just to be sure."

Sure? Sure of what?

"The woman's down there now. Husband's parking the car. We'll bring him straight back."

But you knew, didn't you: their kindly lie? You knew.

The couple. The couple who'll be taking him. From the university, they said. A couple from the university.

VANESSA Tom and me.

TOM Me and Vanessa.

Scene Five

TOM Me and Doctor Vanessa gorgeous Riley? Didn't think I stood a chance.

VANESSA Tom Nielsen? I did. The moment I saw him, I did.

TOM I'd go and listen to her lecture – maths – sneak in at the back.

VANESSA I'd see you.

TOM Bright as a star and more tricks than a circus. And afterwards, that time:

VANESSA Woodstock Road.

TOM Telling you I lectured part-time in musical composition and performance and that I did concerts.

VANESSA What do you play?

TOM The piano, and things.

VANESSA And things.

TOM Well, the piano.

VANESSA When's the next one.

TOM Concert? Next Tuesday, St Hilda's. Seven-thirty. But I also play pubs.

We'd come to my road. You walking away backwards, laughing. Me stood still, wanting to go with you.

VANESSA Bye-bye, piano man.

TOM Watching you go.

Did she turn up? No. But then lo and behold, three weeks later, playing at The Feathers and in she glides, all slow and graceful like a rich man's yacht, looking a million dollars. In fact looking like two million dollars.

VANESSA So here you are, piano man.

TOM Here I most certainly am, Duchess. Great lecture the other day by the way: "The language of maths". Fantastic.

VANESSA Tell me what you were really doing there, Mr Nielsen.

TOM Well, you tell me, how else was I going to get to sit and look at you for almost an hour without getting myself arrested?

It was all a whirl after that, a dance. And didn't we dance – weeks, months of it.

And then that Sunday – late afternoon and still in bed, asking her to marry me and her asking me why.

VANESSA I don't *do* anything, Tom.

TOM Because, I love you. And as for not doing anything, if you were a newly-painted wall, I'd watch you dry.

Both our mums came. We had the upstairs room at The Feathers. And me, I'd never been happier, not ever in my life. Bliss. Acres of it, getting better every day.

Then that night, from out of nowhere:

VANESSA Listen, Tom. What can't you hear?

TOM Everything between the things I can hear.

VANESSA No, no, listen.

TOM Told me to imagine myself walking through each room, standing at the top of the stairs, in the hallway, picture myself sitting in the kitchen.

Nothing.

VANESSA Babies. You can't hear any babies. And I want us to hear them, Tom. I want the noise and life of them filling this house.

TOM It was as quick and as simple as that: couple; family.

So when she telephoned me from the doctor's to tell me that she was pregnant:

Really?

VANESSA Really.

TOM I remember it seeming the most amazing and at the same time the most obvious thing I'd ever heard.

All the toys, getting a room ready, a cot, our mums coming round. And her face, the way she seemed to glow, you know? Brighter every day. Like there was nothing that could shine more brightly, nothing that could put that light out.

Nothing.

The pain in her back and the stomach cramp, that's what woke her.

When I came back from phoning the ambulance she had moved to the far side of the room, sitting up against the wall. The sheet she'd wrapped round herself dark and slack with the bleeding.

So when she returned that day from the clinic to tell me she was pregnant again, I felt, forgiven, you know: second chance.

This time she stayed in bed. She would sleep. And I would tell her, every day I'd tell her that she looked so well, that I could feel the way the baby had grown.

VANESSA Impossible, Tom.

TOM But I could. I could feel the way it had grown.

There were new toys, a different cot. We'd bought them but we hadn't fetched them home, not just yet.

The first check-up.

She called me from the clinic.

VANESSA Fine, everything's fine.

TOM Everything?

VANESSA Everything, Tom.

TOM The second check was scheduled for an afternoon: two-thirty. I'd arranged a taxi. It was to wait then bring them both home.

Then bed.

VANESSA I'm not an invalid.

TOM Please.

They called, remember – the clinic. Said it might be for the best if I came over.

Why best? What best?

Said they'd like to keep her in.

She had on one of those pale-blue gowns that do up the back. They'd let her listen to the heart beat.

So quiet, she told me, the little heart. She couldn't believe how quiet it was. They said I might even hear it too if I put my ear against her.

VANESSA Try. Cover your other ear.

That's it.

Can you?

Can you hear him, Tom?

Tom?

TOM Later, after she'd gone back to work, people were, polite.

Whenever I was asked to come and collect her from a lecture or seminar, the reason was always that she had become, "unwell".

Never that she had been crying, never that she had stopped talking mid-sentence and was just stood staring.

Found her like that once. They'd called me and I'd found her just like that, standing at the far end of an empty lecture room.

Ness?

And that way she turned suddenly, as though startled, angry almost, until she seemed to notice who it was.

VANESSA It's all right. It's all right, Tom. Just. I was just –

TOM Home now, Nessa. Yes?

VANESSA But what are we going to do, Tom? No babies. No babies, piano man.

Scene Six

KATHLEEN The couple. The couple who'll be taking him;

Just to be sure, Kathleen. That's all.

We'll bring him straight back.

The woman's down there now.

But you knew, didn't you: their kindly lie? You knew.

No one came. No one said.

They let you keep the clothes.

Scene Seven

VANESSA Yes, just arrived, thank you. No, very easy. I've brought the clothes to put him in: a shawl, the other things in your letter – everything. Yes, in a parcel at the front desk.

Imagine, I told the people in the shop: "My sister's had a little boy."

Name? We've chosen, Charlie. Tom's father was called—

My name? Sorry. Vanessa Nielsen. No, not "mrs", Doctor. Doctor Vanessa Nielsen. I work at the – my husband? Yes. Tom, he's, the car, yes.

A few minutes? That's fine. Thank you.

Charlie.

I'll tell you all about this one day. When you've grown up and gone away and come back to visit me. I'll tell you what it was like sitting here in this hallway waiting for them to bring me another woman's baby – waiting for them to bring me you.

See her, Charlie? The one with the parcel of clothes – your clothes – walking up the wide staircase? There, stopping at a door along the landing: knocking, going in, not quite closing it behind her. Voices.

CHARLIE Who's—? What did you hear?

VANESSA Through that gap in the door.

CHARLIE Her voice?

VANESSA But not the words, Charlie. Can't hear the words.

CHARLIE What was it like, the voice?

VANESSA Just the sounds.

CHARLIE What was she like?

VANESSA You'll ask me that: "What was she like?" You'll want to know. You'll want to know everything. I've read that: they will want to know everything. And you must tell them.

And I will, Charlie. I'll tell you all this.

But I'll keep the rest – all the questions, all this asking myself: when will I know? When will I become certain that he's really mine, certain that he's become more than someone I've been lent rather than given?

When does that happen?

I'll keep that.

Scene Eight

BILL Pouring out there. Got off the wrong stop. Soaked through.

VANESSA We came by car.

BILL Wrong stop.

VANESSA My husband's—

BILL Come for my little girl, Kathy. Thought she'd be down here waiting. They said she'd be—

VANESSA Well, I think they bring them. It's what they told me: to wait here.

BILL They don't know I've turned up though.

VANESSA No.

BILL It's just she should be here. They said. They told me: down here waiting, ready.

Scene Nine

KATHLEEN So which kiss was the last? Which desperate hug with my face cuddled down in his? There was no struggle. But you knew, didn't you: their kindly lie.

No one came. No one said. They let you keep the clothes.

I haven't cried, not for years, not really, not until his second letter – ten days ago – the one with the photographs. Then that sense of shock I'd placed inside myself for the cold comfort of its numbness, that I'd put there between me and the things that had happened, broke and fell away like bricks in a floodwall. And oh, I cried then; felt myself tugged and dragged at by the sobbing till I ached, but still I cried, hugging at the photographs.

And I cried for me. I cried for him and all our lost times. But most of all I cried for the faces of my mum and dad I saw cradled deep within smiling faces of his children.

Scene Ten

BILL They told me: she'd be down here, ready, that I could fetch her home.

VANESSA I'm sorry?

BILL It's what they said.

Going to ask. Find someone and ask them.

VANESSA And then she's smiling at me and smiling down at what she's holding wrapped in the patterned shawl we'd bought especially.

Feel my arms lifting, reaching out. And oh, here you are.

Taking you. Your gentle fingers gently curling at the patterned shawl. Your perfect lips, your hair. Wanting to touch. Those wide deep eyes. Charlie?

CHARLIE Mum.

VANESSA Hopeless. Don't understand my crying.

CHARLIE It's all right.

VANESSA It often happens, I hear someone saying – the crying. It's all right.

He's brought the car to the front, they tell me: your husband.

Handing you back briefly to fasten my coat. Watching as they take you outside.

Thank you. Thank you so much.

From where I stand in the hallway I can see you out there on the top step, you and the woman in the grey uniform holding you, waiting for me as I do up my coat.

I watch your rimpled face through the frosted glass as the one in uniform holds you, swaying, patting you gently. The late-afternoon cold lifting at the patterned shawl, snow-white against the greyness of the woman's jacket. Charlie swaddled in snow. Charlie, wide-eyed and staring back at me across the grey shoulder, back into the hallway.

But then not at me.

Past me.

Charlie?

CHARLIE Mum?

VANESSA You aren't looking at me at all.

CHARLIE Mum, what are you—

VANESSA You're looking up past me, up into the silence behind the door at the top of the stairs that they've fetched you from. You are, aren't you?

CHARLIE Mum, what are—

VANESSA Can feel it.

CHARLIE What?

VANESSA There. Can almost touch it: like a thread running and tugging between you both.

CHARLIE Who?

VANESSA Between you and that woman behind the door at the top of the stairs. Can't you see it?

CHARLIE There's nothing—

VANESSA As though at that very moment, at the very point of separation, its length and strength for the coming years were being tested.

CHARLIE There was never—

VANESSA Running between you – mother and son, mother and son – always running between you, always there, no matter where or how far away I try to take you.

CHARLIE I didn't. I never looked. I never—

VANESSA When? When do I begin to feel all right? When do I start to have permission?

And I can feel it all about to happen: the panic that I get in lectures sometimes and they have to call Tom. All breathing quickly, wanting to run. Wanting to—

Want to run up those stairs, up each step. Hammer with my fists till the door swings back into the room and I'm standing there, shouting at her:

Charlie's mine, he's mine now. Let go. Please, for Christ's sake, let him go. Just let him—

But there'd be no one there, would there? Just some child; some child sitting on the edge of a narrow bed, awkward – both of us so awkward. Both of us—

God. I was really - I was going to just - Charlie.

CHARLIE It's all right.

VANESSA —felt myself almost - God.

Fasten your buttons now. That's it. Breathing. That's it. Ready now.

Reaching out to take you from the woman in the grey uniform.

Ready now.

Ready now.

Last night I sat listening to Tom playing in the other room.

CHARLIE Dad.

VANESSA Dad. And I thought of this moment, now. This walking down these steps towards the car. This first ride home to the house you'll grow up in, where everything is ready, waiting to begin. Where, one day, when I'm an old lady, you'll tell me—

CHARLIE —it was all right, you know. We were all right.

VANESSA You'll tell me that, won't you, Charlie?

CHARLIE I will.

I did.

VANESSA You see, last night I was imagining all this: holding you tight all the way back, feeling your little body sigh and flicker in its sleep, your breathing gently timing in with mine. Imagined myself telling you: time to come home now, Charlie. I wonder if you'll remember me saying that: time to come home.

You see, I didn't think I could – come here today, I mean – not really. Wasn't sure I even should. Who was I? Another woman's baby? Who was I? But here I am.

Together now, down these wide grey steps to the car and home. You and me.

CHARLIE You never met her?

VANESSA To talk to? No.

CHARLIE Only, I'd always imagined some sort of hand-over – that you'd met her then.

VANESSA No.

CHARLIE Did you want to?

VANESSA You'll ask me that.

And then – inevitable really – but one day, when you'll have taken me out somewhere perhaps – a day you'll have built yourself up to, wondering where the words would come from – you'll ask me how I'd feel about you maybe trying to trace her: your birth mother. That's what they're called: birth mother – how I'd feel.

And, for my sake you'll use the word, "trace", sensing that "search" might sound too full of need; for my sake.

And for your sake, I'll somehow find a way to tell you that you must.

Scene Eleven

KATHLEEN So now this, his last letter – Tuesday: no photographs, no, but lots of asking, wanting to see you.

Friday. Would Friday be all right?

Friday, yes.

I cleaned the house, then yesterday I cleaned it all again. Sat hot and suddenly shaky at the bottom of the stairs, the side of my head against the banister rail.

Today. One hour. Him, coming here. Imagine.

You would go out to eat, he'd said.

CHARLIE Would love to take you out.

KATHLEEN You were to choose the place and he would book the table. But shouldn't there be something when he first arrived, tea or beer? He was coming a long way: London. There ought to be something.

This morning I bought some beer.

London.

So now.

I sit looking in at myself before the bedroom mirror, something tight mixing with the excitement – checking for the hankie in my sleeve.

What will he think? This last letter unsettled me. The language, the words he used. You could tell the sort of education they'd bought for him. And I could almost hear an accent and hear the way that it was quite different from my accent. What would he think of me? What will he think?

And there'd be questions, things he'd want to know. There'd be blame. Yes he'd be pleased to see me, to take me out, but there'd still be blame. There's always blame. You read that. Always.

I could show him the clothes, his clothes. But why? That would be silly: baby clothes. He'd think you were silly.

Nothing to show him.

What will he think of me, Dad?

What will he think?

Scene Twelve

BILL I've just been told. The new people, they've only just fetched the baby. It's only just happened.

I thought it would have all been over with long before now, that Kathy'd be sitting down here in the hall, ready, waiting for me, her case all –

KATHLEEN There was a delay, Dad. Didn't they say?

BILL Waiting.

KATHLEEN Staffing – I thought you knew.

BILL If I hadn't gone off asking questions, looking for her. If I hadn't gone off, I'd have been sat here and seen the whole thing, seen them bring – seen them—

And I wouldn't have known who they were either. Wouldn't have realised that this was the couple. I wouldn't have known. Grandson. I'd have seen him and I wouldn't have known – that close.

It would have happened in front of me without me knowing.

Was that? That was her, wasn't it, the woman I spoke to? That was her.

Right. Right then. Doesn't matter. Something else. Talk about something else, quickly. Stopped raining? I think it has. I think it's probably stopped by now, don't you?

Just been up. To see her: Kathleen; Kathy – see how she was. Went to ask. They said I shouldn't. Leave her to come down herself, they said, when she felt ready. But how would she've known that it was all right to come down, that I wanted her to come down, if I hadn't gone up there?

KATHLEEN I needed to know—

BILL That it was all right, settled now between us – her and me. And I needed to know.

Going up? Course I'm going up, I'm her dad.

And opening the door. Christ.

Sat there in her coat. Suitcase. Parcel of clothes – they're going to let her keep the clothes. Everything folded, clean.

All right, love? Kathy?

Couldn't look at me. Then when she did, when she turned to me, her face, I felt everything inside me just, I felt—

All done, then, love?

Her face, just looking at me the same way she'd looked the day I found out.

Right then. Well, I'll be downstairs. All right?

Put my hand out, touched her shoulder. And her hand, reaching up to keep me there, pushing her thumb under my fingers as though she would have hidden her whole self under them if she could.

That's it. There now.

Stayed like that, still, till she took her hand away and pushed the parcel of clothes along the bed towards me. Not looking, just pushing at the parcel, wanting me to take it away.

Be downstairs then.

Had to go up there. I'm her dad. How else would she have known?

There'll be no forgetting. It's all right. We've been spoken to. Told. I know all about the importance of "getting on with things". But there'll be no forgetting all this. That's what was there on her face when I went up just now.

Best to live alongside it, you might say, if you can.

Haven't described it to anyone else like that: living alongside things. June, my wife, she'd call it being soft if she knew. "Wallowing". It's what she'd say.

There'll be no names, no addresses, photographs. We're not to ask. I know that. The social worker – she's explained all that.

KATHLEEN It was all part of getting on with things, Dad.

BILL She'll arrange with the new people to visit the baby over the first few weeks. Just to check, to be sure. Then when she visits us, we'll be able to ask her how he's getting on.

KATHLEEN Settling in.

BILL We're not to ask any more than that, just how he's getting on. That's the understanding. That's what I agreed to. We're not even to try. She'll visit them and then she'll visit us. We can speak to her about him then.

KATHLEEN Could be the same day.

BILL I've thought about that: same day; her seeing him and talking with them about how he's growing, how he's starting to notice things.

KATHLEEN Sounds and faces.

BILL Starting to smile.

KATHLEEN Even after a few weeks.

BILL And then she'll visit us.

KATHLEEN Starting to smile.

BILL And after that, after those few weeks, all that'll stop. No more visits. We have to be prepared for that, she said.

KATHLEEN Like giving him away all over again.

BILL So we'll need to listen to her. Take it all in: what she tells us – everything. Because that's all we'll have. Once it's over and the visits stop, that's all we'll have to keep. We'll have to imagine the way—

KATHLEEN —he went on changing, developing.

BILL And I'll probably wonder what he'll keep of us and what he'll take on from them, the new people.

KATHLEEN Looks.

BILL Not just looks, I mean his character—

KATHLEEN —and who he took after, who he's like.

BILL There'll always be traces of this family, won't there? Something of us left, mixed in between the layers of whoever he becomes.

Forget all this?

Stopped raining.

We'll go on then, won't we, Kathy? And we'll manage. And this quiet between us'll disappear.

It's only been the quiet of people not wanting to disturb things because there's been too much disturbance already; that's all it is.

Not sure I've had the words up till now anyway. Maybe it was just easier not to try. Maybe that's it. People do what's easiest.

Scene Thirteen

KATHLEEN Your dad.

It's all the memory you have of him now.

So. This. Ten minutes. Parking somewhere now, I expect. Getting out of his car, looking at the houses. Looking at this house.

My face feels – it feels like, I don't know.

I don't really, I don't really think I can. Not now. Not today.

Raking up the past like that. Silly. I must have been –

What was I –

You'll have to phone, tell him. Now, phone him now.

You were very sorry, but he'd have to understand. It just wasn't convenient at the moment – today – it just wasn't. You were very sorry – all that way, I know. You were so sorry.

You were not to worry, he'll tell you – don't worry. He'll phone and cancel the table.

CHARLIE Right away.

KATHLEEN It wasn't a problem. You were to leave it all to him.

Another time?

Of course, yes, another time. Lovely. Another time.

Goodbye then.

Yes, goodbye.

Goodbye.

The relief as you gently replace the receiver.

The relief.

That's probably why you don't respond at first when the doorbell rings, why you simply get up – lifted almost – and go out onto the landing, why you don't even bother to check yourself in the mirror, for the hankie in your sleeve.

The stairs. Across the hall. Faster now, rushing and trying not to rush – you and your beating heart.

The rimpled shape of him through the frosted glass.

Your fingers trembling the lock, pulling back the door.

Oh, you.

Lights fade.

End

This one-woman monologue version of the text, first performed on BBC Radio 4 by Victoria Gould, was the basis from which the stage play was developed.

And so, today: two hours. Imagine, him coming here.

You still have the clothes, don't you; the ones they let you keep? Still in that drawer in the upstairs room, and the piece of faded blue card with his birth-weight and the time – blue for a boy. The letters are in there too.

You. You broke your mother's heart, you did. Fifteen years old. The shame. The way she said it, it sounded like a plague. You were an angel fallen from grace, clattering to the ground with the same sound as all those grinny-toothed, school-uniform photos she'd gone round the house turning over, slamming down – jagged glass across the paleness of your face. The shame.

That was the morning she found out, remember? She didn't guess; she knew. How many weeks late? Look at me; how many? Dragging at your arm to turn you round, hurting you. You were never easy. And now this. This. Fifteen. Well you're going to get rid of it, Kathleen.

And there were your father's sad eyes, slowly pulled away when you met by awkward chance upon the stairs, or if he came suddenly into a room he'd thought was empty. Remember how the opening door would shock you back from your dreaming down amongst the gas-fire colours, your shoulders hunching forward, hands fumbling in your lap to hide the slowly-changing shape of you. See him stand there for a moment, hesitant, as though wanting to speak, as though wanting for you both to speak as you had always done, but now neither of you able to find the words.

He'd sigh then, wouldn't he – turn back out the room more slowly than he had entered it? Your dad. That's all the memory you have of him now, that sad slow turning away.

Shame and sadness.

Shame and sadness became the places they retreated to then; separate, silent places. There was no rage. No bitter kitchen-table nights. Rage would have made it easier. Too easy. Rage would have given you something to rage against.

But instead: her unforgiving, hall-clock silence pointing at you as you moved from room to room, its cold finger pressed tight across your lips.

Quiet now; we'll say no more about it. It's all forgotten.

So it was agreed, arranged. Remember the day: whispered voices in the hallway; the sound of a car. You would only be gone for a short while. A holiday, that's what we'll say. You've gone to your aunt's for a holiday.

And later, years later, when you had moved away and come back alone to pack her things – after the funeral – it was still there, that same tight-lipped struggle for a self acceptance she called respectability. There in the anxious precision of the dried-flower arrangement, in the order of the animals made of glass. It was there in the correctness of things.

Well that was why it had happened, wasn't it: the thought of being incorrect; the excitement of it? But it was so awful. That boy.

Some lad I hardly knew – some army lad. There was something hurried about him that shocked me. It was as though by having finally said, "yes", I'd reduced to nothing the very thing he'd spent so long waiting for, and turned it into something best done with quickly. And in that moment where I thought I'd find a sense of being wanted, there was only the wanting for him to finish.

Somehow I'd spoilt it. He didn't say so, but that's what I'd done. You were never easy, and now this. This.

And after, everything crushed – the grass, my clothes. The dress is new, I told him. He said he thought he was in love.

Some lad I hardly knew – some army lad—

There are houses built there now.

The little clothes. Sometimes I'd go into the upstairs room, just to look, to touch. It's where I put the letters, next to the piece of faded blue card with his birth-weight and the time – blue for a boy.

The letters.

I thought the first one was some sort of children's charity appeal – I knew the language well enough – *I am writing on behalf of a friend who is trying to trace a relative with whom he has lost touch.* I was all set to throw the silly thing away, remember, my mind already gone on to other things? Then I saw the date, the name of the town. This town.

My hand pushed tight across my mouth as though about to be sick, trembling.

Not me. No. They don't mean me. Just a coincidence, that's all. Just a stupid. The page fluttering in my fingers like something caught.

Can't be. Mustn't.

Angry with myself, ashamed. As though by wondering about him all those years – all that: *Today he's one year old.* And, *September: he'll be starting school this week. Today he's twenty-one* – by wondering about him, I'd somehow brought all this about, this disruption, this, this interference.

And the hardest one: *Does he ever think of me?*

And he did. He does. Thirty years.

I replied, terrified, curious – yes, I told the social worker, the friend could write if he wanted to. No, I didn't know how I'd respond.

And the awful waiting.

His first letter. Three weeks, last Wednesday.

I'd somehow expected the writing to be like a child's – big felt-tipped letters sprawling my address. Not this, this man's writing.

Didn't open it at first, couldn't; just smoothed at the envelope as though the letters were in braille, the way I'd smoothed his hair, his cheeks. The feel of it. Can't be.

How odd, writing to you, he said. And I wrote back: odd, yes.

My dry tongue as I tried to lick the stamp. The catching in my stomach as I let the envelope fall away down into the letterbox. Wanting to run home. Feeling the years fall back. Feeling the years fall in on me. Wanting to cry.

It seemed the only thing to do then, didn't it, as soon as I got home; the only place to go? I sat on the floor of the upstairs room by the open drawer and for the first time I let it come back to me. Staring out across those years, I dared let it all come back to me again: the milky warmth; the tiny sleepy softness of him; those wide deep eyes holding me. Mine. The only time I'd ever really been in love, I told myself. All mine.

And after the birth, those six short weeks of them bringing him in to be fed. Six weeks of them coming to take him away again, and my heart with him.

And then the day they didn't come for him – not straight away. That's how I knew: it will be today. Now. Giving me time. They were telling me by giving me time – warning me. And suddenly, suddenly so much to say to you; a lifetime of telling, of asking and listening. But still I never finished – oh, as if I ever could have finished.

There was no struggle. "We don't want him woken now, Kathleen," they told me. "Need to show him to the couple who'll be taking him; just to be sure. That's all. We'll bring him straight back."

But you knew, didn't you: their kindly lie? You knew.

So which kiss was the last, which desperate hug with my face cradled down in his?

So quiet after the door had closed – whispered voices in the hallway; the sound of a car. No one came. No one said. They let you keep the clothes.

I didn't cry, not for years, not really, not until his second letter, the one with the photographs. Then that sense of shock I'd placed inside myself for the cold comfort of its numbness, that I'd put there between me and the things that had happened, broke and fell away like bricks in a floodwall. And oh, how I cried then; felt myself tugged and dragged at by the sobbing till I ached, but still I cried, hugging at the photographs.

And I cried for me. I cried for him and all the lost times. But most of all I cried for the faces of my mum and dad I saw cradled deep within smiling faces of his children.

So now this, his last letter – Tuesday: no photographs, no, but all this asking, wanting to see you.

Friday. Would Friday be all right?

Friday, yes.

I cleaned the house, then yesterday I cleaned it all again. Sat hot and suddenly shaky at the bottom of the stairs, the side of my head against the banister rail.

You would go out to eat, he said. Would love to take you out. You were to choose the place and he would book the table. But shouldn't there be something when he first arrived, tea or beer? He was coming a long way: London. There ought to be something. This morning I bought some beer.

London.

So. Now.

I sit looking in at myself before the bedroom mirror, something tight mixing with the excitement – checking for the hankie in my sleeve.

What will he think? This last letter unsettled me. The language, the words he used. You could tell the sort of education they'd bought for him. I could almost hear an accent and hear the way that it was quite different from my accent. What would he think of me? What will he think?

And there'd be questions, things he'd want to know. There'd be blame. Yes, he'd be pleased to see me, to take me out, but there'd still be blame. There's always blame. You read that. Always.

I could show him the clothes, his clothes. But why? That would be silly: baby clothes. He'd think you were silly.

Nothing to show him.

What will he think? What will he think of me, Dad?

So now. Ten minutes. Parking somewhere, I expect. Getting out of his car, looking at the houses. Looking at this house.

My face feels – it feels like. You know, I don't know. I don't really think I can. I don't want. Not now. No. Not today. Raking up the past like that. I must have been.

You'll have to phone, tell him. Now, phone him now. You were very sorry, but he'd have to understand. It just wasn't convenient at the moment – today – it just wasn't. You were very sorry – all that way, I know. You were so sorry.

You were not to worry, he'll tell you – don't worry. He'll phone and cancel the table. Right away. It wasn't a problem. You were to leave it all to him. I'll take care of everything.

Another time?

Of course, yes, another time. Lovely. Another time.

Goodbye then.

Yes, goodbye.

Goodbye.

The relief as you gently replace the receiver.

The relief.

That's probably why you don't respond at first when the doorbell sounds, why you simply get up – lifted almost – and go out onto the landing, why you don't even bother to check yourself in the mirror, for the hankie in your sleeve.

The stairs. Across the hall. Faster now, rushing and trying not to rush – you and your beating heart.

The rimpled shape of him through the frosted glass. Your
fingers trembling the lock, pulling back the door.

Oh, you.